21st
Century
Skills Library

COOL ARTS CAREERS

MUSIC PRODUCER

PATRICIA WOOSTER

CHERRY
LAKE
Publishing

Published in the United States of America by
Cherry Lake Publishing, Ann Arbor, Michigan
www.cherrylakepublishing.com

Content Adviser

Paul Farahvar, President and CEO, Shoeshine Boy Productions, Chicago, Illinois

Credits

Cover and page 1, ©iStockphoto.com/track5; page 4, ©V&A Images/Alamy;
page 7, ©Tetra Images/Alamy; page 8, ©Alexey Fursov/Shutterstock; page 10,
©Aija Lehtonen/Dreamstime.com; page 13, ©AP Photo/Richard Lewis; page 14,
©Stepanov/Shutterstock; page 15, ©Lucian Milasan/Dreamstime.com; page 16,
©Arvind Balaraman/Shutterstock; page 19, ©auremar/Shutterstock; page 21,
©Brain A Jackson/Shutterstock; page 22, ©Yakov Stavchansky/Dreamstime.com;
page 24, ©Pavel Losevsky/Dreamstime.com; page 25, ©Aaron Settipane/
Dreamstime.com; page 26, ©Lisa F. Young/Shutterstock; page 28, ©AP Photo/
Dan Steinberg

Library of Congress Cataloging-in-Publication Data

Wooster, Patricia.
 Music producer/by Patricia Wooster.
    p. cm.—(Cool arts careers)
 Includes index.
 ISBN-13: 978-1-61080-133-1 (lib. bdg.)
 ISBN-10: 1-61080-133-4 (lib. bdg.)
 1. Music trade—Juvenile literature. 2. Sound recordings—Production
and direction—Juvenile literature. I. Title.
 ML3795.W575 2012
 780.23—dc22   2011001582

Cherry Lake Publishing would like to acknowledge
the work of The Partnership for 21st Century Skills.
Please visit *www.21stcenturyskills.org* for more information.

Printed in the United States of America
Corporate Graphics Inc.
July 2011
CLFA09

TABLE OF CONTENTS

MUSIC PRODUCER

CHAPTER ONE
UNDERSTANDING MUSIC PRODUCING

A new band's dream is coming true as the musicians enter the studio with their instruments and get

Producer George Martin helped the Beatles become one of the most successful rock groups of all time.

ready to play. The band is recording its first album after months of playing small shows. The audio engineer and the producer are in the control booth to record and adjust the sounds. The producer gives direction for each song and helps the band members create a vision for their album. He may ask them to speed up a song, take the pitch higher, or change the lyrics. He guides the musicians as they try to create a hit record. After the recording session, the engineer and the producer still have work to do. They use audio equipment and computers to make the recordings sound as good as they can.

One of the most famous and successful producers of all time is George Martin. In 1962 he began working with a group of four unknown musicians called the Beatles. The Beatles went on to sell more than 1 billion records and to become one of the most popular bands of all time. Martin encouraged them to try new sounds and music styles. He helped them to develop as artists and to push themselves forward with each album. During his career, Martin produced 19 number-one hit albums and 22 number-one hit singles in the United States. His production talent inspired many young people to enter the music business.

Today, technology plays a key role in the music industry. People **download** music from the Internet and store it on computers and portable devices. Musicians of all ages and skill levels can record their music and post it online for others to hear. People interested in music production can buy affordable home studio equipment and learn to record and mix songs.

Technology is changing how music is heard and produced. Everyone has access to an audience through the Internet.

Josh Swade is a music producer and the owner of a small record label. He produces and markets new artists. When Swade was growing up, his father played the drums and was passionate about music. "When I was in high school, I bought a pair of turntables and began to DJ at parties and events," Swade says. He decided to pursue a career in the music business.

LEARNING & INNOVATION SKILLS

Thomas Edison invented the phonograph in 1877. This invention was the main recording technology for many years. In 1925 the electronic microphone improved the sound quality of recordings. By the early 1980s, records were also available as cassette tapes and compact discs. Today, music can be downloaded from the Internet and carried around on a tiny music player.

In the past, people could only hear music on the radio, at a concert, or on a record purchased at a store. Most people only listened to music created by professional artists. Now anyone can record music at home and put it on the Internet. How do you think this affects the music industry?

Vinyl records are just one of the many ways to listen to music today.

Producers often play several roles in the music business. Some sign artists to recording contracts. Many are involved in songwriting and completing final **masters** of songs. They work closely with audio engineers, who use technology to enhance music and polish the final sound.

Audio engineers are an important part of the recording process.

Some producers help their artists with public relations. They might arrange live performances or hire a director to make a music video. Producers might also decide on the best time to release an album, to make sure it sells well. They use **branding** to create public images for their artists. They also work with **blogs**, Web sites, and magazines to help get the word out. Some producers help artists with everything from musical direction to business decisions. Others work only on the musical side of things.

Most small independent production companies have fewer resources than larger companies. This means independent producers must take on many roles. Artists **copyright** their songs. This means other artists cannot record the same song without permission. Producers make arrangements with record companies, television producers, and movie companies to **license** songs. Some production companies provide music for video games, commercials, and animation. They may spend a lot of time in meetings trying to gain new business for their artists.

Music producers work with creative people. They meet new artists and watch current artists try new things. They do so many things that every day is different. How would you like to listen to a record you produced or see a concert you helped organize?

CHAPTER TWO
A DAY ON THE JOB

Producers work with a lot of musicians and might work on many projects at the same time. It is important for them to be flexible. Every client has different needs.

Live performances help musicians find new audiences.

Marketing is a very important part of the job for some producers. They create marketing plans to help promote the release of a new album and spread the word about the artist. These plans cover publicity, promotion, production, touring, advertising, and budgets. Different people work on each part of a plan.

After a marketing plan is in place, a music producer deals with radio stations and the media to help promote the artist. Interviews, articles, and radio play are all important tools for spreading the word about new music. Many producers today also use social media such as Facebook and Twitter to promote their artists. Social media lets fans communicate directly with the artist and share links with one another. It's a great way to have a conversation with many people at one time. It can also help to quickly spread news about a new musician.

Producers help musicians create material, too. A producer and musician may brainstorm ideas for new songs or albums. They often spend a lot of time together during recording sessions. They work as a team to perfect songs and complete them on schedule.

Bands go on tour to perform in front of live audiences around the world. This gives musicians a chance to connect with their fans and gain new listeners. Producers might work with their artists' managers to schedule and promote tour dates.

Sometimes producers might be in charge of finding **venues** for the concerts. Producers may even handle travel arrangements and hotel reservations for smaller acts. Musicians usually go on tour after they release a new album. They use the concerts as a way to promote the new music.

21ST CENTURY CONTENT

In February 2010 Apple Inc., announced that more than 10 billion song downloads had been sold through its iTunes store. iTunes is the most popular online store for music and movie downloads. The music can be played on computers, home stereos, and portable devices.

New technology allows people to do more and more with their electronic devices. Many people today own cell phones, computers, and portable music players. Some also own several other devices. Almost all of these devices can play music. New inventions will continue to let people listen to music wherever and whenever they want.

Apple's Steve Jobs has helped to make iTunes a major success in the music industry.

Music producers sometimes work with managers and agents to promote a band's tour. They do their best to let people know where and when the band is performing. Producers or promoters send **press releases** to local newspapers and radio stations announcing the band's tour information.

Press releases include information about the dates, locations, and where to buy tickets. Radio stations that play the band's music are good places to advertise upcoming concerts. Tour information is also placed on the band's Web site, various fan sites, and message boards.

Each project that a producer works on has a budget. Producers need to keep track of spending for each part of a project. They must spend only what the budget allows. This helps keep projects profitable.

Radio DJs can help spread the word about upcoming concerts.

Social networking sites such as Twitter have become an important way to spread information about musicians.

Producers need all these skills and more to make it in the music industry. They need to be able to do many things at once and be able to quickly adjust their plans. Making music can be a tough, fast-paced business!

CHAPTER THREE
BECOMING A MUSIC PRODUCER

Music production is a competitive business. You should start learning as early as you can if you want to succeed. Listen to many different types of music.

Learning about music can help you become a good producer.

Learn to recognize the sounds of different instruments. Pay special attention in your math classes. Producers need math skills to work on budgets, accounting, and **royalties**.

You can also begin producing your own music with an in-home studio. Many new computers come with built-in recording programs that you can use to practice. You can use the Internet to share and promote your music.

Home production software and recording equipment have become more affordable in recent years. You can use them to edit, mix, and master music. This will help you learn more about the recording process.

You can also go online to find out about new kinds of music and see what is popular. Many Web sites allow you to sample new music for free. Try listening to classical, country, jazz, and other types of music. Many producers specialize in a certain style of music. To do that, you need to know which styles you like best. Pay attention to the music in movies and commercials. Music is everywhere, so you have a lot of chances to hear new things.

A college degree can be helpful in becoming a music producer. College students have access to the newest technology and recording equipment. A bachelor's degree in music can provide education in recording, music theory, and business. Some producers attend audio engineering schools to learn how to work in a studio. Courses in accounting, marketing, and public relations will help with the business side of the job. So will public speaking and management skills.

LIFE & CAREER SKILLS

According to the Institute for Policy Innovation, the music industry loses $12.5 billion every year due to online piracy. The Recording Industry Association of America (RIAA) thinks this illegal downloading is the reason that music sales have gone down in recent years. The RIAA often files legal charges against people who are caught downloading music illegally.

Musicians are not the only people affected by pirated music. Producers, sound engineers, and record stores lose money and jobs when music sales are down. What do you think should be done to prevent online piracy? What can the music industry do to help?

An **internship** is a great way to get experience in the music industry. Interning at a production company will let you work directly with producers. Interning at a promotion company, concert venue, or record label can also provide valuable experience and **networking** opportunities. Internships allow you to see different sides of the music industry and decide what kind of work you want to do.

Interns learn important business skills from experienced professionals.

There are many employment opportunities for music producers. The average salary for a music producer is $64,430. Salaries vary widely depending on the type of production and the success of the artists. As the music industry continues to shift toward a digital future, there will be greater demand for producers who know how to use new technology. Producers work with musicians, songwriters, and audio engineers. They also deal with businesspeople such as promoters, publicists, and lawyers. Producers must be able to communicate well with all of these people.

Education and experience help prepare you for a job as a producer. But a love of music is even more important. "If you have passion, you can compensate for a ton of other areas you may not be so inclined to grasp," says Josh Swade. "You need persistence and patience because you will likely have to pay your dues. It usually doesn't happen overnight."

Producers should learn everything they can about the process of creating music.

CHAPTER FOUR
A FUTURE IN MUSIC PRODUCING

The music industry is always changing. Artists and producers continue to push things forward. New technology

Producers need to stay up to date with new recording technology.

has changed the way artists are marketed. It has also changed the way music is recorded, packaged, and sold. It is easier than ever for fans to access new music and discover new artists. The Internet has made this possible. Music can be downloaded at any time of day from anywhere in the world. Many people have stopped buying compact discs completely. Their music collections are fully digital.

21ST CENTURY CONTENT

Audio engineers are an important part of the recording process. They can change the sound of a singer's voice. They can add instruments or other special effects. They use audio equipment and computer software to control the recording.

Recording technology used to make musicians sound worse than they did in real life. Producers struggled to capture their musicians' talents. This is no longer the case. New technology allows engineers and producers to make an artist's recordings sound better than they really are. Do you think technology should be used to fix poor performances?

Companies such as Disney and Nickelodeon make stars out of teens who can sing, dance, and act. Their talents are used to sell television series, movies, albums, and merchandise to their fans. Their careers are built by business managers and marketing plans. They make a lot of money for their companies. Some go on to have successful careers as adults.

Producers help artists figure out how to develop their music in interesting new ways.

The careers of pop stars such as Miley Cyrus are carefully controlled by their producers and managers.

You can keep up with changes in the music industry by reading industry news, joining professional organizations, or attending networking events. You may want to take classes to learn more about certain subjects. Technology will continue to change. It is very important to keep your skills sharp.

The National Association of Record Industry Professionals (NARIP) is a nonprofit organization for people who work in the music industry. It holds events to spread information about different aspects of the business. You can visit these events to learn about music development, financing, social media, and other subjects. They are also a great way to meet new people. NARIP and other organizations post internship and employment opportunities. These organizations can be a valuable resource.

Classes are a great way to keep up with new developments in the music industry.

No matter how things change, people will always love music. Josh Swade says that the best part of his job is "working with creative, interesting people from very different backgrounds." In the future, music producers will continue to develop new talent and create **trends**. Their desire for new sounds and recording methods will help drive the creation of new technology. Will you be one of the creative people who help push the music industry forward?

LEARNING & INNOVATION SKILLS

According to the Guinness Book of World Records, the Beatles song "Yesterday" has been recorded more than 1,600 times by different artists. It has been covered by musicians from different genres and enhanced with computer technology. A music producer can alter the sound of a song by introducing new instruments or by changing the vocals or the song's tempo. A producer sometimes takes an old song and updates it for a new generation of listeners. "Yesterday" was first recorded in 1965. More than 45 years later, musicians and producers are still adding their personal touches to the song! Think of a song from the past that you like. What changes would you make to modernize it for today's audience?

THE ASCAP FOUNDERS AWARD
TO

DR. D

PRODUCER
RAPPER
ENTREPRENEUR
ICON

ASCAP

Producers such as Dr. Dre have help shape the sound of modern pop music.

SOME FAMOUS MUSIC PRODUCERS

Dr. Dre (1965–) revolutionized hip-hop in the late 1980s with productions for his group N.W.A. He later went on to discover and produce superstars such as Snoop Dogg, Eminem, and 50 Cent. He has won six Grammy Awards and sold millions of records as both an artist and a producer.

Steven Epstein (1951–) produces classical music for Sony Music Entertainment. He has won 15 Grammy Awards. He also teaches graduate-level courses in record production at McGill University in Montreal, Canada.

Quincy Jones (1933–) has produced many famous pop albums and has won many awards for his work. Michael Jackson's *Off the Wall* and *Thriller* are two of his most well-known productions. *Thriller* is the best-selling album of all time.

George Martin (1926–) is often called the Fifth Beatle. He has produced more than 50 hit records. He has also won six Grammy Awards, a Novello Award and a Grammy Lifetime Achievement Award.

Timothy Zachery Mosley (1971–) is a record producer, songwriter, and rapper known as Timbaland. He has produced songs for Nelly Furtado, Justin Timberlake, and Katy Perry. He often brings together artists from different genres to create new sounds.

Rick Rubin (1963–) is the president of Columbia Records and a cofounder of Def Jam Records. He is known for producing songs with strong vocals and few computer enhancements. He has worked with Run DMC, the Beastie Boys, the Red Hot Chili Peppers, and the Dixie Chicks.

GLOSSARY

blogs (BLAHGZ) easily updated Web sites used to share short text entries, photos, or links

branding (BRAND-ing) creating a public personality for a company or product

copyright (KAH-pee-rite) to legally protect a creative work or invention

download (DOUN-lohd) to receive files or data over the Internet

internship (IN-turn-ship) a way to gain work experience while being mentored

license (LYE-suhns) to give permission to use copyrighted material

masters (MAS-turz) final recordings that copies are made from

networking (NET-wurk-ing) meeting people to make business connections

press releases (PRESS ri-LEES-ez) official announcements of a new product or event to the public

royalties (ROI-uhl-teez) payments given to artists and songwriters when records are sold or songs are licensed

trends (TRENDZ) styles that are popular for a short time

venues (VEN-yooz) places where shows and concerts are held

FOR MORE INFORMATION

BOOKS

Hilvert, John, Linda Bruce, and Alan Hilvert-Bruce. *Music Technology.* North Mankato, MN: Smart Apple Media, 2006.

Miles, Liz. *Making a Recording.* Chicago: Raintree, 2010.

Throp, Claire. *Digital Music: A Revolution in Music.* Chicago: Raintree, 2011.

WEB SITES

All Music
www.allmusic.com
Use this valuable resource to keep up with new music and learn about different musical styles.

Association of Music Producers
www.ampnow.com
Learn more about music industry events and educational opportunities.

Billboard.com
www.billboard.com
Follow music industry news and check the charts to see what artists and songs are most popular.

21ST CENTURY SKILLS LIBRARY

INDEX

ABOUT THE AUTHOR

Patricia Wooster has a degree in creative writing and psychology from the University of Kansas. She lives with her husband and two sons in Tampa, Florida.